LEADERS TRANSFORM
THE ART OF INFLUENCE

Book 1:
Begin with Self Transformation

HUGH BALLOU

Published by SynerVision Publishing

© Hugh Ballou.

No part of this publication may be reproduced, stored in a retrieval system, or transmitted, in any form, or by any means, electronic, mechanical, photocopying, recording, or otherwise, without the prior consent of the publisher

CONTENTS

The Leader's Journey Begins Within 1
Authenticity & Integrity 7
Vision and Self-Awareness 15
Mindset and Confidence 21
Continuous Learning and Habits 27
Balance and Self-Care 33
Action Plan – Becoming an Unbound Leader 39
Conclusion 43
Lead from the Inside Out 43
Summary Chapter 49
Leading from the Inside Out 49
Appendix I: Transformational Leadership 53
Appendix II: More Resources by Hugh Ballou 59

CHAPTER 1
THE LEADER'S JOURNEY BEGINS WITHIN

> *" Leadership is transformation of self, then organization"*
> *Hugh Ballou -*

> True leadership begins not with strategies, titles, or external authority—but with the transformation of the inner self. This chapter introduces the foundational principle of transformational leadership: before we can influence others, we must first lead ourselves. This journey begins not in the boardroom, but in the mirror.

I'm excited to announce a new series called Leaders Transform. If you know me, you know I champion transformational leadership—a style rooted not in power, but in influence.

As a conductor, I held a small baton. That baton didn't give me power to make anyone do anything—it symbolized influence. Skilled, clear leadership invites others into alignment and excellence.

This is a leadership transformation series, and this first volume is about transforming self. Before we can transform others or organizations, we must begin the work within. Leadership is a journey—an ongoing path of improvement—not a destination.

Leadership doesn't start in the boardroom or on the podium—it starts in the mirror. Through my decades of work with executives, clergy, entrepreneurs, and nonprofit leaders around the world, one truth has become clear: transformation starts from the inside.

This book and its companion video and podcast are designed to provide you with practical tools—not theory, not pep talks. You'll find systems and strategies I've used and refined over four decades as a conductor, church leader, business consultant, and leadership coach.

SynerVision is the name of my company, because vision is at the core of synergy. We must be clear about our vision before we can align others internally and externally. Whether you're new to leadership or seasoned and experienced, this series is here to equip you for confident, decisive leadership.

This is session one, chapter one—The Leader's Journey Begins Within. Leadership isn't about titles or loud voices. It's about influence—and influence is rooted in authenticity, clarity, and discipline.

When I first stepped onto the conductor's podium, I realized musicians watched me for more than cues. They responded to my confidence, posture, energy—even distraction. That moment shaped my understanding of leadership.

Your habits, emotions, and energy ripple into your organization. You cannot inspire excellence in others unless you cultivate it in yourself.

Leaders want to improve results, performance, and morale. But change doesn't begin with meetings or metrics—it begins with mindset. The culture of your organization mirrors your leadership.

This book will help you define who you are, what you value, and how to align your life with a compelling personal vision. It's not about being perfect—it's about growing in awareness and purpose.

Illustration: The Mirror and the Baton

Imagine a conductor standing before an orchestra. The baton is ready, the musicians are poised, the audience waits. But before a single note is played, the conductor must take a moment—look in the mirror—and reflect: What energy am I bringing? What intention am I setting?

Just like the conductor, every leader must first check in with themselves before attempting to guide others.

Key Practices

- Start the Day with Reflection – Take 5 minutes each morning to check in with your emotions, energy, and purpose.
- Name Your Values – Write down 3 non-negotiable values that guide your life and leadership.
- Track Your Reactions – Pay attention to moments when you feel triggered, reactive, or out of sync. These are opportunities for growth.

Practical Tools & Exercises

Vision Paragraph Exercise:

Write a one-paragraph vision statement beginning with: "The leader I choose to be is..."

Focus on the qualities, mindset, and influence you want to develop—not just the results you hope to achieve.

Mirror Moments Journal:

For the next 7 days, journal your responses to the following:

- When did I feel most aligned with my values today?
- Where did I lead with influence rather than control?
- What personal habit helped (or hindered) my leadership?

Self-Assessment: Inner Leadership Inventory

Rate yourself on a scale of 1(rarely) to 5 (consistently):

Statement	1	2	3	4	5
I begin each day with intention and reflection.					
I can clearly articulate my core values and my guiding principles.					
I stay calm and centered under pressure.					
I recognize when I'm reactive and work to respond with intention.					
My team or peers would describe me as authentic and self-aware.					

Scoring Guide:

5-10: Opportunity for deep self-reflection

11-17: Growing awareness - keep building the habits.

18-25: Strong self-leadership - refine and share your influence

Reflection Questions

- What does "transformation begins with the leader" mean to you?
- How do your current habits impact those around you?
- Where in your leadership are you reacting rather than responding?

- In what ways does your inner world (stress, confidence, values) shape your outer results?

Key Takeaways

- Leadership begins not with others, but with self.
- Influence is more powerful than control—and it begins with authentic alignment.
- Leaders who transform themselves create cultures of excellence, trust, and clarity.
- Your habits, thoughts, and values ripple out into your organization.
- Leadership is not a position; it's a practice.

Next Chapter Preview

Chapter 2: Authenticity & Integrity – Embracing Your True Self

In the next chapter, we explore the foundation of sustainable influence: leading from your true self. Authenticity and integrity aren't optional—they are the source of trust, clarity, and emotional resilience in leadership. Learn how to align your actions with your values, live transparently, and model the kind of character that inspires followership.

CHAPTER 2
AUTHENTICITY & INTEGRITY

"The culture is a reflection of the leader and it responds like an orchestra responds to the subtle nuances of the conductor."-Hugh Ballou

> Authenticity and integrity are not external strategies—they are internal alignments. This chapter explores how being real, honest, and values-driven is not only more sustainable but far more powerful than any polished leadership persona. When leaders embody authenticity and integrity, they gain trust, inspire loyalty, and create resilient cultures.

Authentic leadership isn't about putting on a role—it's about taking one off. Too often, leaders wear a "mask" at work, believing they must act a certain way to gain respect, assert authority, or maintain control. But masks create disconnection. People don't follow titles; they follow people. And people follow leaders who are real.

When I first stepped into formal leadership, I thought I had to become someone else—more commanding, more polished, more "in charge." What I've learned since is this:

authenticity is not a liability—it's your greatest asset. When you lead from your true self, grounded in your values, you radiate clarity and conviction. People are drawn to leaders who are honest, vulnerable, and human. They can trust them.

Trust is the currency of leadership. Without trust, your influence is shallow, fragile, and temporary. With it, you build relationships, movements, and organizations that last. And trust begins with authenticity.

There's a myth in leadership that you must always have the answers, always look strong, never show doubt. That's exhausting—and it's false. True leadership is not about perfection. It's about alignment. When your actions reflect your inner values, you become someone others believe in.

Let me be candid: early in my leadership journey, I sometimes tried to project confidence when I felt uncertain. I masked doubt with bravado. But over time, I discovered that I became more confident not by pretending, but by anchoring myself in clarity, service, and transparency. Once I led from my core, I didn't need to perform. I could lead from purpose.

If authenticity is the foundation, then integrity is the structure. Integrity means your life is in rhythm—your values, your words, and your actions are in sync. In music, a conductor must maintain a consistent rhythm and emotional tone. Any deviation—no matter how subtle—can cause the orchestra to falter.

Leadership works the same way. When your behavior shifts with circumstance or convenience, when you say one thing and do another, your team notices. And when they notice inconsistency, trust erodes. Your leadership influence falters, like an ensemble out of tune.

But when your leadership is rooted in integrity, your people know what to expect. You become a stabilizing presence, especially in moments of uncertainty. Integrity doesn't mean perfection—it means consistency. It means owning your decisions, acknowledging mistakes, and showing up aligned every time.

Being authentic doesn't mean oversharing or being unfiltered. It means being anchored. It means knowing who you are and leading from that place without apology or façade. People don't need you to be perfect—they need you to be present and real.

Your team can sense when you are centered. Your voice, your decisions, your body language—all of it communicates alignment. When they feel your authenticity, they respond with greater openness and trust. They engage not because they have to, but because they believe in you.

Key Practices

- Practice daily self-check-ins to assess whether you're acting from your true self.

- Name and define your core values—use them as a decision-making compass.
- Share your leadership challenges with a trusted peer or mentor to break the illusion of needing to be perfect.
- Admit mistakes openly and model responsibility without shame.
- Use feedback as a mirror to assess alignment between how you see yourself and how others experience you.

Practical Tools & Exercises

Authenticity Alignment Exercise:

Write about a time when you felt most like yourself in leadership. What conditions made that possible?
Then write about a time when you felt you had to perform. What beliefs were driving that behavior?
What would it look like to bring more authenticity into your daily leadership?

Self-Assessment: Authenticity & Integrity
Rate yourself on a scale of 1(rarely) to 5 (consistently):

Statement	1	2	3	4	5
I lead in a way that aligns with my values and guiding principles.					
I am honest about what I know and what I don't know.					
I am consistent in my actions, regardless of who is watching.					
I take responsibility for my mistakes without deflecting blame.					
People describe me as transparent and trustworthy.					

Reflection Questions

- Where in your leadership are you most authentic?
- Are there areas where you wear a "mask" or feel the need to perform?

- What core values do you want to align more fully with your actions?
- What's one behavior you can adjust to bring your leadership more into integrity?

Key Takeaways

- Authenticity is not a liability—it is your greatest leadership asset.
- Trust begins with being real, not with being perfect.
- Integrity builds confidence in your leadership by creating predictable behavior.
- People follow leaders they believe—not just leaders who perform.
- Alignment between values, words, and actions builds lasting influence.

Final Thought

Authenticity and integrity are not leadership tactics—they are the essence of who you are as a leader. In the orchestra of leadership, these qualities form the tuning pitch. Get that right, and everything else begins to resonate.

Remember: Leaders Transform—and everything changes. And it starts with you.

Next Chapter Preview

Chapter 3: Vision and Self-Awareness – Crafting a personal vision and increasing emotional intelligence.

The journey continues by diving into the power of self-awareness and the clarity of vision. Discover how emotionally intelligent leaders create teams, organizations, and outcomes that resonate with deep purpose and personal alignment.

CHAPTER 3
VISION AND SELF-AWARENESS

> *"A leader without a vision is like a conductor without a score."*-Hugh Ballou

> Vision gives leadership direction. Self-awareness gives it grounding. In this chapter, we explore how personal vision becomes a compass for daily decision-making, and how self-awareness provides the reflection needed for integrity and alignment. Together, these qualities form the foundation of transformational leadership.

Great leaders, great leadership, all leaders, always begin with a clear, compelling vision. This is how I created center vision. From the vision, we then create the ensemble, the synergy. So, it's the center vision of our work. But here's the truth. Your vision is not just a strategy for others to follow. It's a compass for how you live, how we live.

So, we write a vision, that's how we live and how we'd lead every single day. It's not merely about what you want to achieve. It's about who you choose to become. As I'm writing this book, I'm thinking about my first book. And I wrote the chapter, Getting Things Done First, out of a bunch of chapters, which was my vision for completing the book. So, writing it down and committing to it was the first step in, here's the vision, and here's how we get it done.

When I first stepped into leadership roles, I believed that vision was about crafting statements for teams or organizations. But since I've learned the most powerful vision isn't something you place on a wall. It's something you carry in your heart, your spirit, in your very being.

A leader's personal vision defines their internal identity, not just their external impact. It informs our tone, our presence, our priorities. It gives our leadership depth and resilience. Because when we know who we are, we know what we stand for. We're not easily swayed by circumstances.

Your personal vision answers these questions:

- What kind of leader do I want to be?
- What values guide my decisions?
- How do I want others to experience my presence?

Without that clarity, leadership becomes reactive. With it, leadership becomes magnetic.

Vision without self-awareness is like trying to steer a ship in the fog. You need to see yourself clearly before you can lead others clearly. Self-awareness is what brings vision to life. It keeps us honest, present, and emotionally attuned.

Through my decades of coaching and conducting, I've seen a recurring pattern. Leaders who lack self-awareness often confuse intensity with influence. While they may be brilliant in strategy, they are tone deaf in relationships. And it costs them trust, morale, and momentum.

Self-awareness is not just knowing your skills and gaps. It's the ability to observe your impact in real time. It's the discipline of reflection and the humility to seek feedback and the willingness to shift when needed. That's why the best leaders journal, meditate, assess their energy and cultivate emotional intelligence.

As a musical conductor, I quickly realized that I couldn't hide behind the music. That was a major revelation for me. My mood, posture, and energy were cues to the musicians following instinctively and intentionally. If I was tense, that translated to them. They tightened up. If I was grounded, they relaxed and performed at their best. It's like unleashing the passion, the purpose. That's what leadership is—leading the tone before the team ever hears the words.

When our vision and our self-awareness align, something extraordinary happens. Your leadership gains congruence. Our words match our actions. Our presence aligns with our purpose. People trust us because we are the same person in the boardroom, in crisis, and in our one-to-one conversations.

That's when our leadership begins to transform others—because we are already transformed from the inside.

Key Practices

- Write your personal leadership vision and revisit it weekly.
- Create space for daily reflection to monitor your alignment with your values.
- Ask trusted colleagues for feedback on how they experience your presence.
- Track your emotional energy throughout the day to identify patterns.
- Align your calendar and priorities with your stated vision and values.

Practical Tools & Exercises

Crafting Your Leadership Vision:
Write a one-page personal leadership vision. Address:

- Who you want to be as a leader
- The core values that ground you
- The impact you want to have on others
- The legacy you aim to leave behind

Use present-tense language. Speak as the leader you are becoming.

Self-Assessment: Vision and Self-Awareness

Rate yourself on a scale of 1(rarely) to 5 (consistently):

Statement	1	2	3	4	5
I have a written personal leadership vision that guides my decisions.					
My daily actions reflect my core value and guiding principles.					
I actively seek feedback and reflect on my leadership impact.					
I remain emotionally aware and centered under pressure.					
Others experience my consistently across different contexts.					

Reflection Questions

- What personal vision guides your leadership journey today?
- Are there gaps between how you see yourself and how others experience you?
- In stressful situations, how do you typically respond—and what does that reveal about your current level of self-awareness?

Key Takeaways

- Vision provides direction. Self-awareness ensures alignment.

- A leader's internal identity shapes their external influence.
- When vision and self-awareness are in harmony, leadership becomes magnetic.
- Clarity and emotional intelligence build trust and resilience.
- Your leadership tone begins with your presence, not just your words.

Next Chapter Preview

Chapter 4: Mindset and Confidence – How developing a growth mindset and internal confidence changes the way you show up and influence others.

We now shift focus to how mindset and confidence shape your posture, presence, and power as a leader. Learn how to step into your role with assurance and lead forward with belief and boldness.

CHAPTER 4
MINDSET AND CONFIDENCE

"The willingness to fail and learn from that failure is a fundamental leadership skill."-Hugh Ballou

> Mindset is the internal engine of leadership. Confidence is the fuel. In this chapter, we unpack how your thoughts shape your beliefs, and how those beliefs drive your leadership presence. By identifying limiting beliefs and cultivating a growth mindset, leaders begin to lead not from fear, but from faith, purpose, and preparation.

Leadership begins with the mind. It's in the mind first, and then it's manifested. Before we ever speak a word, make a decision, or cast a vision, we are already leading by the way we think. Your thoughts shape your beliefs, and those beliefs shape your behavior. As a result, if you believe you aren't capable, ready, or worthy, you will lead from limitation. But when you cultivate a mindset of growth and confidence, you unlock the ability to lead with boldness, clarity, and resilience.

Many leaders carry invisible barriers, unspoken doubts, inherited narratives, or inner critics that whisper things like, you're not enough. I've heard them as well, constantly. In my early transition from conductor to leadership coach, I often ask myself, "Who am I to guide CEOs, pastors, entrepreneurs, and other leaders?" But eventually, I realized something important. The stage may change, but the principles remain. As a conductor, I learned to lead without having to say many words, using presence, precision, and preparation to draw excellence from others. I began to see that those same skills could orchestrate transformation beyond the concert hall. The only barrier was my own mindset.

Some research on mindset brought to light the truth that many great leaders discover. Some people believe their abilities are fixed. It's a fixed mindset. While others believe abilities can be developed. The Growth Mindset. The growth-minded leader sees every challenge as a chance to grow. Every failure is feedback. Every obstacle as an invitation to rise. I don't see failure. I see those things that I didn't do right as a learning opportunity. And obstacles turned around become opportunities. The mindset continues how we frame those challenges into opportunities.

This mindset fosters ability, creativity, and resilience. All of these are vital leadership traits in a fast-changing world. Those remain constant. It also creates space for others to grow. When a model of growth is the mindset, the team will follow.

Confidence doesn't magically appear. It does not magically appear. That's important. Doesn't appear when you step into this leadership role. It's not pretending or puffing yourself up. True confidence is rooted in purpose, consistency, and preparation.

The more you align your daily actions with your values and long-term vision, the more grounded you become. I'm speaking to myself in that. doing this a long time, I still speak to myself. I learn with every one of these that I do. And when we're grounded, people can trust us. Confidence becomes the by-product of integrity and action, not ego.

I remember a moment on the podium standing before a 100-piece orchestra. I had rehearsed every single part of this piece, every cue, every breath. But the most powerful moment wasn't in the preparation. It was in the stillness before that first downbeat.

In that moment, all the eyes were on me, not to control, but to guide. My confidence wasn't in a title. It was in the clarity of my intention and the strength of my presence. Leaders don't need to have all the answers. Leaders need to stand in purpose and invite others to rise with them by asking good questions and listening carefully to the answers. You've heard that before. You'll hear it again.

Key Practices

- Name your limiting beliefs and reframe them into empowering beliefs.
- Practice gratitude and self-acknowledgment daily to reinforce confidence.
- Treat setbacks as feedback—not as failure.
- Align your thoughts, words, and actions to your values and vision.
- Visualize leadership success before key moments or decisions.

Practical Tools & Exercises

Rewriting the Inner Script:
Step 1: Identify one limiting belief you currently hold.
Step 2: Write an empowering statement to counter it.
Step 3: Speak it aloud daily for 21 days. Belief follows repetition.

Example:
Limiting belief: "I'm not experienced enough."
Empowering belief: "Every day, I grow into the leader I am becoming."

Self-Assessment: Mindset and Confidence

Rate yourself on a scale of 1(rarely) to 5 (consistently):

Statement	1	2	3	4	5
I approach challenges as opportunities for growth.					
I recognize and counter my own limiting beliefs.					
I take action even when I feel uncertain.					
I speak to myself with encouragement and purpose.					
My confidence grows from consistency not comparison.					

Reflection Questions

- What beliefs are currently limiting your leadership potential?
- When have you experienced growth after stepping through discomfort?
- How would your leadership shift if you believed more deeply in your ability to grow?

Key Takeaways

- Leadership begins in the mind, not the meeting.
- Limiting beliefs shrink your influence—growth beliefs expand it.
- Confidence is a byproduct of action, integrity, and preparation.

- Growth mindset transforms failure into feedback and setbacks into success.
- Bold, grounded leaders inspire trust and unlock potential in others.

Closing Thought

Your mindset sets the ceiling for your leadership. But when you choose to grow, the ceiling disappears. You don't have to be fearless—just faithful to the process. The next chapter explores how to stay committed through routines, rituals, and lifelong learning.

Next Chapter Preview

Chapter 5: Continuous Learning and Habits – Building routines for growth and excellence.

Sustainable leadership is not built on occasional inspiration—it's built on daily intention. In Chapter 5, we explore how habits, rhythms, and lifelong learning keep leaders grounded, growing, and effective over time.

CHAPTER 5
CONTINUOUS LEARNING AND HABITS

> *"Transformation is not a destination, it is a continuous process of growth and refinement."*
> *-Hugh Ballou*

> Leadership excellence is not achieved once, but rehearsed daily. This chapter focuses on continuous learning and intentional habits as the engines of growth. By modeling curiosity, humility, and discipline, leaders create cultures where transformation is expected and sustained.

Excellence in leadership isn't achieved once and for all—it's cultivated through a commitment to continuous growth. In my years working with high-level leaders, one truth has become unmistakable: The best leaders are not those with all the answers. They're the ones who ask the best questions. They are students—of themselves, their craft, their teams, and the world around them.

Think of leadership like conducting. A musical conductor doesn't stop learning once the score is memorized. Each rehearsal reveals new dynamics. Each performance deepens interpretation. The same piece of music can unfold differently depending on the day, the players, and even the mood. A skilled conductor embraces this fluidity and grows with it.

Leadership, similarly, is not static. Every conversation, decision, or challenge offers an opportunity to reflect and adjust. Great leaders stay sharp by adopting the mindset of a lifelong student—constantly refining their influence, their communication, and their impact.

Lifelong learning begins with humility—the understanding that there's always more to learn, and that today's success does not guarantee tomorrow's excellence. It means being teachable. Leaders who model humility and curiosity create cultures of innovation, reflection, and trust.

Continuous learners:

- Ask thoughtful questions
- Read widely and reflect deeply
- Invite and act on feedback
- Seek out mentors and coaches
- Embrace discomfort as a signal for growth

Learning doesn't require dramatic shifts. In fact, the most powerful growth often happens through small, consistent efforts. Set aside time each week to learn—read a leadership book, listen to a podcast, attend a webinar, or debrief your wins and mistakes.

Habits are the architecture of leadership growth. Grand visions are only realized through small, repeatable actions. Intentional leaders design rhythms into their lives—like a morning routine, weekly review, or regular journaling practice—that strengthen focus and alignment.

Consider this: A violinist doesn't wait until the night before a concert to practice scales. They rehearse daily. Likewise, leadership habits compound over time, building capacity, resilience, and clarity.

Ask yourself:

- What small actions could I build into my day to elevate my leadership?
- Which distractions do I need to eliminate or reduce?
- Am I building leadership muscle, or simply reacting to each day?

Leaders who neglect growth risk stagnation. In today's rapidly changing world, yesterday's solutions won't solve tomorrow's challenges. Failing to evolve limits your ability to inspire, innovate, and lead effectively. Worse, it sets a ceiling for your team.

But when you model continuous learning, you empower your team to grow with you. You create a culture where excellence is expected, not just encouraged.

Key Practices

- Dedicate time daily or weekly to learning and reflection.
- Maintain a humble, teachable spirit—recognize you never 'arrive.'
- Debrief both successes and failures for growth opportunities.
- Model learning habits for your team by sharing your process.
- Replace distractions with practices that fuel your vision and growth.

Practical Tools & Exercises

Design Your Leadership Growth Rhythm:
Set a weekly schedule for your learning and reflection. Consider including:

- Daily: 10–15 minutes of journaling or reading
- Weekly: 30 minutes reviewing wins, challenges, and growth opportunities
- Monthly: One learning activity (course, book, or coaching session)
- Consistency builds capacity.

Self-Assessment: Continuous Learning & Habits

Rate yourself on a scale of 1 (rarely) to 5 (consistently):

Statement	1	2	3	4	5
I dedicate regular time to intentional learning.					
I reflect on my successes and failures to identify growth lessons.					
I maintain daily or weekly routines that support my leadership.					
I invite feedback and use it constructively.					
I model continuous learning for those I lead.					

Reflection Questions

- What are the top 3 habits that currently shape your leadership?
- When was the last time you intentionally learned something new about your leadership style?
- What does your current schedule say about your commitment to personal growth?

Key Takeaways

- Leadership is a rehearsal, not a performance—it requires ongoing learning.
- Small, consistent learning habits create significant transformation over time.

- Humility and curiosity are the bedrock of lifelong learning.
- Habits compound and become the architecture of leadership excellence.
- Neglecting growth sets a ceiling not only for you but also for your team.

Closing Thought

Leadership is not about staying ahead of others—it's about staying in motion. A learning leader becomes a transforming leader. Let your habits reflect the leader you're becoming, not the one you've been.

Next Chapter Preview

Chapter 6: Balance and Self-Care – Maintaining energy and boundaries for sustainable leadership.

In the next chapter, we explore how leaders can sustain energy, manage stress, and establish boundaries. Balance and self-care are not indulgences—they are essentials for resilient, long-term influence.

CHAPTER 6
BALANCE AND SELF-CARE

"Leaders who neglect self-care will eventually lead from a place of depletion and not inspiration."-Hugh Ballou

> Balance and self-care are not luxuries—they are leadership essentials. This chapter explores how managing energy, setting boundaries, and practicing intentional self-care sustain influence over the long term. True leadership is not about burnout—it is about resilience, clarity, and presence.

Sustainable leadership isn't about doing more—it's about doing what matters most with presence, purpose, and peace. Leadership isn't just about external results. It's also about your internal reserves. You can't serve from an empty vessel. You can't lead others to clarity if you're in a fog of fatigue.

Over the years, I've coached hundreds of leaders—from CEOs and entrepreneurs to clergy and nonprofit directors—and I've seen a troubling pattern: many high-performing leaders run on empty. They mistake exhaustion for excellence, chaos for commitment, and burnout for proof of hard work. But let's be clear: burnout is not a badge of honor.

It's a flashing red light—warning you that you're out of alignment.

Too often, we think of balance as a perfect distribution of hours across every area of life. That's unrealistic—and unhelpful. Balance isn't about splitting your day into neat quadrants. It's about aligning your energy with your values. It's about choosing what gets your best, not just what gets your time.

Balance means learning to say no without guilt. It means putting margin into your calendar—time to reflect, rest, and recalibrate. It means recognizing that your leadership capacity expands or contracts based on how well you care for yourself.

Here's what I've learned: when I'm rested, nourished, and centered, I make better decisions. I communicate more clearly. I lead more effectively. But when I'm depleted, everything feels like a crisis—even when it's not.

Let's bust a myth right now: Self-care is not selfish. It's one of the most strategic leadership tools you have. Your presence—how you show up emotionally, physically, and spiritually—sets the tone for your team or organization.

Self-care doesn't have to be complicated. It might include:

- A consistent morning routine

- Movement or exercise
- Time in nature or silence
- Reading for pleasure or growth
- Prayer, meditation, or journaling
- Taking a true day off each week

Whatever restores you, schedule it with the same priority as your meetings. Don't treat rest as optional—it's essential.

Strong leaders set strong boundaries. That means defining your availability, protecting your focus time, and modeling a healthy pace for your team.

Remember: every time you say yes to something, you're saying no to something else. If you always say yes to urgency, you'll say no to vision. If you say yes to everyone else's needs, you may say no to your own family, health, or purpose.

Boundaries are not barriers—they are bridges to sustainable leadership.

As a conductor, I learned that pauses in the music are just as important as the notes. They give space for breath, reflection, and impact. The same is true in leadership. Your pauses create power.

The question is not just "How can I be more productive?" but "How can I be more present, purposeful, and whole?" True leadership doesn't demand your burnout—it requires your well-being.

Key Practices

- Schedule rest and renewal as non-negotiables in your calendar.
- Define and communicate boundaries for availability and focus.
- Identify your energy drains and prioritize activities that restore you.
- Practice saying no to good things so you can say yes to the best things.
- Model balance and self-care as an example for your team.

Practical Tools & Exercises

Create Your Personal Energy Map:

Over the next 7 days, track your energy levels at regular intervals (morning, midday, evening). Note what activities preceded low energy and what preceded high energy. Look for patterns. Adjust your schedule to maximize your energy peaks and protect your recovery times.

Self-Assessment: Balance and Self-Care

Rate yourself on a scale of 1(rarely) to 5 (consistently):

Statement	1	2	3	4	5
I schedule time for rest and renewal consistently.					
I set and maintain healthy boundaries in my leadership role.					

Statement	1	2	3	4	5
I am aware of what restores my energy and make time for it.					
I model balance and self-care for those I lead.					
I notice early signs of burnout and address them proactively.					

Reflection Questions

- What does a balanced week look like for you—realistically?
- What are your top 3 warning signs that you're nearing burnout?
- What restorative practices are missing from your routine?
- How do you currently model self-care to those you lead?

Key Takeaways

- Balance is not about equal time—it's about aligned energy.
- Self-care is a leadership strategy, not a luxury.
- Boundaries create the freedom for sustainable influence.
- Leaders who model rest and renewal empower teams to thrive.

- True leadership requires wholeness, not depletion.

Leadership Insight

As a conductor, I learned that pauses in the music are just as important as the notes. They give space for breath, reflection, and impact. The same is true in leadership. Your pauses create power.

Next Chapter Preview

Chapter 7: Action Plan – Becoming an Unbound Leader – Creating a personal transformation plan guided by the Four Leadership Principles.

In the final chapter of this book, we put everything together into a personal leadership transformation plan. Grounded in authenticity, vision, confidence, learning, and balance, you'll map a path forward to lead with influence and integrity.

CHAPTER 7
ACTION PLAN – BECOMING AN UNBOUND LEADER

"The missing element in most failed plans is implementation, so strategy without action is just a speech."-Hugh Ballou

> This final chapter is about moving from reflection to implementation. Transformation only becomes real when it is put into practice. Here, you'll create your personal leadership action plan—your blueprint for becoming an Unbound Leader who leads with clarity, influence, and freedom.

Transformation without action is merely aspiration. No matter how inspired you feel or how much clarity you've gained, nothing truly changes until you take action.

In the previous chapters, you've explored essential dimensions of leadership: authenticity, vision, mindset, self-awareness, habits, and balance. You've reflected deeply and challenged yourself to grow. But now it's time to put it all into motion.

In my experience as a conductor, transformation in an ensemble didn't happen during the concert—it happened in the rehearsal hall. That's where clarity was built, trust was formed, and intentionality was sharpened. The same is true in leadership. The magic isn't in the performance—it's in the daily practices that prepare you to show up as your best self.

An Unbound Leader is someone who leads with freedom, clarity, and purpose. You're not driven by ego or trapped in outdated models of control. You are grounded in your values, fueled by vision, and energized by growth. You lead from the inside out, unshackled by fear, perfectionism, or performance anxiety.

Being an Unbound Leader doesn't mean you have it all figured out. It means you're committed to the journey, anchored by principles, and open to continuous learning.

The SynerVision Leadership Model: A Framework for Transformation

The SynerVision Leadership Model is built on Four Core Leadership Principles:

- **Foundations** –
    - Who are you?
    - What do you stand for?
    - What vision fuels your leadership?

- **Relationships** –
    - How do you connect and communicate?
    - What do others experience in your leadership presence?
- **Systems** –
    - How do you execute your vision?
    - Are your routines aligned with your highest priorities?
- **Balance** –
    - How do you maintain your clarity and well-being?
    - What boundaries and rhythms protect your effectiveness?

When these four principles are aligned, you gain traction. When one is neglected, everything suffers.

Key Practices

- Revisit your personal vision regularly and refine it as you grow.
- Commit to consistent habits that align with your vision and values.
- Prioritize balance by integrating self-care and boundaries.

- Strengthen key relationships by investing time, attention, and trust.
- Design systems that support your goals and reduce unnecessary friction.

Practical Tools & Exercises

Complete the Unbound Leader Blueprint:

Use the Four Leadership Principles (Foundations, Relationships, Systems, Balance) to design your personal transformation plan. Write it out, keep it visible, and revisit it often. Consider mapping out daily, weekly, and monthly practices that anchor your leadership.

Self-Assessment: Becoming an Unbound Leader

Rate yourself on a scale of 1(rarely) to 5 (consistently):

Statement	1	2	3	4	5
I act daily in alignment with my personal vision.					
I actively strengthen and repair key relationships.					
I maintain systems that support my goals and priorities.					
I protect my energy and balance with intentional boundaries.					
I implement my leadership insights into consistent practice.					

CONCLUSION
LEAD FROM THE INSIDE OUT

"The conductor creates and ensemble of excellence which means creating synergy through a common vision."-Hugh Ballou

> The conclusion brings together the central themes of this book: leadership begins within. True transformation is not about charisma, control, or position—it is about alignment, integrity, and intentional growth. This final reflection equips you to carry forward the discipline of self-leadership into every area of influence.

You've taken the first—and most important—step in transformational leadership: turning inward.

In this book, we've explored what it truly means to lead from a place of authenticity, clarity, confidence, and sustainability. We've challenged old assumptions about leadership being about control or charisma. Instead, we've uncovered a deeper truth: leadership is an inner discipline before it is an outer role.

True leadership begins not on the stage, at the boardroom table, or behind a title—it begins in the mirror.

You've reflected on your vision. You've examined your mindset. You've evaluated your habits, your energy, and your values. And you've begun building a leadership foundation rooted in integrity, self-awareness, and intention.

Let me remind you: self-transformation is not a one-time event. It is a daily practice. A posture of humility. A willingness to grow, to listen, and to evolve.

It's not about perfection—it's about alignment. Alignment between who you are, what you value, and how you lead.

YOUR COMPASS FOR THE JOURNEY AHEAD

Principle	Guiding Reminder
Foundations	Stay grounded in your purpose and vision
Relationships	Build trust and foster meaningful, clear connections
Systems	Align your actions with your mission and eliminate distraction
Balance	Protect your energy and honor the boundaries that sustain you

Let these principles guide you you through each season of leadership. Return to them whenever you feel stuck, overwhelmed, or out of alignment.

Key Practices

- Anchor your leadership in authenticity and self-awareness.
- Revisit and refine your personal vision regularly.
- Protect your energy through self-care and balance.
- Foster strong, trust-based relationships in all contexts.
- Translate clarity into consistent action through systems and habits.

Reflection Questions

- How will you continue practicing daily self-leadership beyond this book?
- Which of the Four Leadership Principles most needs your attention right now?
- How will you celebrate progress and sustain momentum as you grow?

Key Takeaways

- Leadership is an inner discipline before it is an outer role.
- Alignment, not perfection, is the hallmark of transformational leadership.
- The Four Leadership Principles (Foundations, Relationships, Systems, Balance) provide a compass for sustainable growth.

- Self-transformation is an ongoing rhythm, not a one-time event.
- Leading from the inside out transforms not only organizations, but lives.

What's Next?

The journey doesn't end here. This first volume focused on the inner journey—the essential, foundational work of self-leadership. The next book in the Leaders Transform series will turn our attention outward—into leading teams, shaping culture, and creating momentum through influence.

Final Thought

Before you move ahead, take a moment to celebrate.

Celebrate the questions you've asked.
Celebrate the clarity you've gained.
Celebrate the transformation you've begun.

Because here's the truth: The leader who leads with integrity, clarity, and courage doesn't just manage organizations—they transform lives.

That's the kind of leader the world needs. That's the kind of leader you are becoming.

Stay committed.

Stay courageous.
Stay unbound.

— Hugh Ballou

SUMMARY CHAPTER
LEADING FROM THE INSIDE OUT

"The conductor's job is to make the music come alive through others and leadership is no different" -Hugh Ballou

This summary brings together the key themes and practices from the first six chapters of Book 1: Begin with Self-Transformation. It highlights the essential insights every leader needs to embrace to lead with influence, integrity, and confidence. Think of this as your quick-reference guide for continued growth and application.

Chapter 1: The Leader's Journey Begins Within

- Leadership begins in the mirror—your inner world shapes your outer impact.
- Influence is rooted in authenticity, clarity, and self-discipline.
- Transformation is first personal, then organizational.

Chapter 2: Authenticity & Integrity

- Authenticity is your greatest leadership asset—people trust leaders who are real.
- Integrity means consistency—your values, words, and actions must align.
- Trust is the currency of leadership, built on honesty and transparency.

Chapter 3: Vision & Self-Awareness

- A leader without vision is like a conductor without a score—vision provides direction.
- Self-awareness ensures alignment and prevents blind spots.
- When vision and self-awareness converge, leadership becomes magnetic.

Chapter 4: Mindset & Confidence

- Mindset is the foundation—growth mindset turns challenges into opportunities.
- Limiting beliefs are the invisible barriers to influence—replace them with empowering truths.
- Confidence is earned through preparation, integrity, and purposeful action.

Chapter 5: Continuous Learning & Habits

- Leadership is a rehearsal, not a performance—growth requires continuous practice.
- Habits are the architecture of transformation—small, consistent actions compound.
- Lifelong learners remain humble, curious, and resilient.

Chapter 6: Balance & Self-Care

- Balance is not about time management—it's about energy alignment.
- Self-care is a strategic leadership tool, not a luxury.
- Boundaries create freedom for sustained impactful leadership.

Chapter 7: Action Plan – Becoming an Unbound Leader

- Transformation without implementation is just aspiration—action turns vision into reality.
- The SynerVision Leadership Model (Foundations, Relationships, Systems, Balance) is your blueprint for growth.
- An Unbound Leader leads from clarity, courage, and alignment—unshackled by fear or ego.

Final Thought

Leadership is not a destination—it is a lifelong practice of growth, reflection, and alignment. Use this summary as a compass to keep your journey focused. Revisit the principles often and let them guide your daily actions. True transformation begins within—and expands outward to influence teams, organizations, and communities.

APPENDIX I: TRANSFORMATIONAL LEADERSHIP

"The definitive leader is a Transformational Leader."-Hugh Ballou

> Transformational Leadership, rooted in the work of James MacGregor Burns and Bernard Bass, has been shaped by both educational systems and the military. At its core, it is about more than authority or charisma—it is about equipping people, creating community, and inspiring trust.
>
> Transformational Leaders serve the vision they articulate by building community through integrity. They embrace teams, committees, and boards, guiding them toward meaningful participation and shared accountability. Process becomes the unifying force—building trust, creating synergy, and sustaining collaboration.

Traits of a Transformational Leader

1. Clearly articulate vision and goals
2. Define tasks others can do and empower them
3. Develop leaders within teams
4. Delegate effectively

5. Encourage boldness and innovation
6. Provide information and support
7. Affirm and celebrate competence
8. Respect the individual
9. Avoid micromanaging
10. Model what they teach

Transformation vs. Change

To transform is more than to change. Change adjusts; transformation re-forms. Transformation begins with inspiration, but it deepens through action, reflection, and rest.

Like music, true transformation is intentional—it requires both leader and participants to contribute. The sense of ensemble achieved in music applies to all leadership: a synergy greater than the sum of its parts.

Transformational Leadership vs. Charismatic Leadership

- Charismatic Leadership: Centered on the leader's personality; often autocratic, dependent on the leader's presence.
- Transformational Leadership: Centered on the vision; inspires, motivates, and empowers others; builds leaders within the team.

Transformational Leaders model authenticity. Their leadership is not about self but about advancing a shared vision and empowering others to thrive.

Transformational Leaders vs. Charismatic Leaders

"The conductor doesn't make a sound yet leads the ensemble to greatness. Leadership is influence, not control."

1. Core Focus

- Transformational Leader:

Guides the organization with a shared vision. Inspires others to discover their potential. Builds long-term capacity.

"Leadership is creating a culture of excellence by empowering others."

- Autocratic/Charismatic Leader:

Commands attention. Often centers the vision on self. May get fast results but rarely fosters ownership or sustainability.

"Charisma without clarity creates dependency, not leadership."

2. Decision-Making

- Transformational Leader:

Encourages collaboration and collective wisdom. Delegates authority with structure and trust.

"Don't make decisions in a vacuum. Your team is your best resource."

- Autocratic/Charismatic Leader:

Makes decisions unilaterally. May listen, but often dictates final outcomes based on personal intuition or image.

"Speed without synergy leads to burnout and blame."

3. **Role of the Team**

- Transformational Leader:

Sees the team as an ensemble. Each voice matters. Like a conductor, they bring out the best in each player.

"My job as a conductor is not to play the music, but to shape it—through others."

- Autocratic/Charismatic Leader:

Sees the team as followers. Success is measured by loyalty to the leader's charisma or authority.

"Followers perform, but they don't grow."

4. **Sustainability of Impact**

- Transformational Leader:

Builds systems and structures that continue without them. Values legacy and replication of leadership.

"Transformational leadership is scalable because it's not about the leader—it's about the culture."

- Autocratic/Charismatic Leader:

Creates dependency. When the leader leaves, momentum often vanishes.

"Charisma fades. Systems sustain."

5. Culture and Empowerment

- Transformational Leader:

Cultivates trust, growth, and shared responsibility. Operates from purpose, not ego.

"Empowerment is not about giving away power—it's about awakening it in others."

- Autocratic/Charismatic Leader:

Controls the message, the energy, and the spotlight. Team members may feel stifled or invisible.

"When control increases, creativity decreases."

Final Thought

"If the leader is the only one with the music, then the team can never perform without them. Give them the score. Rehearse together. Then step back and let the music soar." — Hugh Ballou

APPENDIX II: MORE RESOURCES BY HUGH BALLOU

Hugh Ballou is a transformational leadership expert, author, and conductor-turned-strategist who empowers leaders to build high-performing teams and purpose-driven organizations.

Orchestrating Success Podcast

Insights on Leadership, Strategy, and Building Impact

Discover how to turn your passion into impact. Each episode provides practical strategies for leading with purpose and influence.

The Nonprofit Exchange Podcast

Empowering Nonprofit Leaders to Thrive, Not Just Survive

Weekly conversations with thought leaders and nonprofit experts offering real-world solutions for growing your mission.

31 Days to Becoming a Better Leader

Daily Reflections for Personal & Professional Growth

A practical guide for leaders who want to grow themselves in order to grow others. Includes short, actionable lessons and reflections.

More Tools, Courses, and Leadership Resources

Visit SynerVision Leadership Foundation to access live workshops, action guides, coaching programs, and more from Hugh Ballou.

LeadForward Magazine

LeadForward empowers purpose-driven leaders by providing insight, inspiration, and tools to lead with influence, integrity, and innovation—helping them make meaningful impact in every sphere they serve.

Books by Hugh Ballou

Get a complete of Hugh's current books which is continuously updated.

Use the QR Code below or this link for all of Hugh's resources – http://HughResources.com

www.ingramcontent.com/pod-product-compliance
Lightning Source LLC
Chambersburg PA
CBHW042345300426
44110CB00030B/173